Afterlife

3 Easy Steps To Connecting And Communicating With Your Deceased Loved Ones

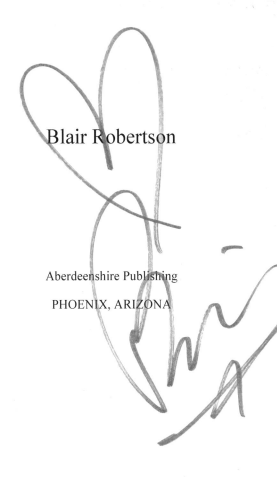

Blair Robertson

Aberdeenshire Publishing

PHOENIX, ARIZONA

Aberdeenshire Publishing
Box 1306
Litchfield Park, Arizona 85340

Afterlife: 3 Easy Steps To Connecting And Communicating With Your Deceased Loved Ones. -- 1st ed.

ISBN-13: 978-1514154472

ISBN-10: 1514154471

For Wendy, the love of my life.

"My message is simple: love never dies"

—BLAIR ROBERTSON

Table of Contents

Welcome!

Hi, I'm Blair Robertson, and I'd like to thank you for purchasing *Afterlife*.

The purpose of this book is simple: to make you more aware of your deceased loved ones in spirit, and to help you make personal connections with them.

Bold claim? It might appear that way. But as a psychic medium I've helped tens of thousands of people just like you from all over the world do just that.

Through my classes and my live demonstrations of mediumship, I have helped people understand that love never dies.

While we all will die at some point, our spirit carries on. Your deceased love ones are near. They want to communicate with you. Unfortunately, in today's hectic world, we often block out the soft and gentle signs they show us. I'm going to help you with that.

As with my previous books, I'm skipping the 'woo-woo' language many other spiritual advisors use. I've designed this book to be as brief as possible and to-the-point.

Spirit communication is subtle. I'm going to show you three easy ways to make connections with your loved ones. I call them the "Three S's: Sleep, Signs, and Silence."

Please *use* the material in this book. Frankly, I think you're wasting valuable time in your life if your only intention is to read it. I wrote this for you to use and to enjoy! I wrote this with the intention of having you making connections with your loved ones on the other side.

I hope you enjoy this book as much as I enjoyed writing it! Thank you, again, and I look forward to hearing of   your   successes!   Onward..

Introduction To Spirit Communication

If there is one thing I hope to sincerely convey to you, it's this: death isn't the end, it's the beginning of another journey.

Your deceased loved ones aren't 'gone.'

Yes, it's true that our bodies will expire at some time. All of us shall pass, but that's just the body.

My favorite analogy is this: when you get a letter from a loved one, what do you do?

You rip open the envelope and eagerly read the letter, don't you? You toss away the envelope, but you keep the letter.

The letter is your soul. Your spirit. The envelope is the container. Our bodies are the envelope; our souls are that letter.

Isn't that a cool way to look at it?

"They are in the next room." Doris Stokes

Your loved ones are near. If they suffered in any way prior to passing, they are all fine and good now, rest assured.

Famed medium Doris Stokes encouraged us to think of our deceased loved ones as being in the next room. It's a comforting thought to know that while you can't see them, they really are still close by.

"But Blair, I'm not a medium! How can I hope to connect with my loved ones?"

Great question. And valid too!

Here's the answer: you don't need to be a medium to make connections with your loved ones on the other side. Each and every one of us can easily make connections. I dare say, we've received them regularly but have likely ignored or missed them.

My loved ones make connections with me regularly.

The difference is that by having the gift of mediumship, I am able to see and communicate with people whom I don't know. Those are your people.

So, you and I are the same. Our loved ones make connections with us regularly. The only way I am different is that I can also receive messages from others that are deceased.

Makes sense, doesn't it? What I am going to be teaching you in this book has nothing to do with mediumship. This is about personal connections with your own loved ones.

Importance Of Spirit Guides

Each and every one of us has spirit guides to help guide us through our lives. I wrote a book on this called *"Spirit Guides: 3 Easy Steps To Connecting & Communicating With Your Spirit Helpers"* that covers this topic in detail.

I'll just briefly point out that your spirit guides are of tremendous importance to helping you become aware of signs and messages. Your guides can also help you make connections with the ones you love.

It's my opinion that your spirit guides are incredibly important to helping you master the connections. To keep this book brief, I'm going to assume that you already have a great connection with your guide or guides.

"Guides Guide, Loved Ones Love."

Blair Robertson

When I speak to groups, one of the biggest aha moments they have is the understanding of the message "our guides guide and our loved ones love."

Many people feel that their deceased loved ones have given up on them because they feel they aren't getting help or direction from them.

This is because the role our loved ones have in the afterlife is to simply love and encourage. It is not their role to guide us... that is the role of our spirit guides.

Example: praying to your deceased mother to help you in a situation isn't going to happen. Doing so only causes you unnecessary frustration. Your guides, however, are standing by ready and willing to help you.

Think of it this way. My nephew is in soccer right now. His coach is his guide. His job is to listen to the direction of the coach, and the coach's job is to help him win. My job is to cheer my nephew on and give him love, encouragement, and support. In other words, it is NOT my role to coach him.

Guides guide. Loved ones love.

Studies show that we get bombarded with more than five thousand advertisements in any given day. They come from emails, web pages, billboards, magazines, bus shelters, radio, television, etc.

Add to that the hectic pace of life, and it's no wonder that we are too busy to hear the soft and subtle messages from our loved ones. No wonder we are becoming a nation of medicated people.

Messages from spirit and our loved ones are very subtle in most cases, and we need to be resonating with that frequency to pick up on them.

How do we 'become one' with spirit? By developing an awareness, and we do that simply through meditation.

"Prayer is talking to God,
meditation is listening to God."

Diana Robinson

I've been using and teaching one of the easiest and most effective meditations ever.

You can do it anywhere, and it's sure to help you alleviate stress and become more aware of spirit.

No, you don't need to wear robes, shave you head, and chant. Well, go ahead and do that if you want to; that's none of my business!

Meditation is one key. The other one – protection from negative energy – is done by invoking white light.

Good news: both are easy, practical to use, and only take a few moments. We'll get to both in the next chapter.

Two Helpful Tips

1. Please understand you cannot force a loved one on the other side to come through. We can't dial them up at any time day or night. They can and do come through at the appropriate times.

I say this because people occasionally think they can just "talk to Mom" any time they wish. Not so.

If they don't come through, it does not mean they hate you. It just means "not right now."

Be patient.

2. I'm going to teach you three different ways to connect. Please try one at a time.

Experience has shown me that, with a sincere effort, you should find at least one technique that will work for you. The sleep connection ceremony, for example, is one that tens of thousands have participated in with me over the years, and it is typically wildly successful.

If it doesn't work after a few tries, try another way. Use what works best for you. There is no right or wrong.

Keep trying. The instructions for each method are purposefully simple and designed to help you connect.

Alrighty, let's move on!

Meditations

To make this book flow a little easier, I'm including two easy meditations that you can use at any time you wish during your day.

If there was a key to success in connecting with your guides, angels, and the highest power of all, it's this: meditation.

After years and years of study, I have come across, without a doubt, the easiest ways to do both.

For simplicity, I have separated them into a white light protection and a breathing/centering meditation. Feel free to combine them.

We will be referencing the breathing meditation all through the book.

How to Protect Yourself with White Light

A lot of people worry unnecessarily about evil spirits, or negative things happening to them when they're connecting with their spirit guides. So let's go back to square one. When you were created, you were created from spirit, from the source, from God – from whatever you call the highest power. So, you are a being of light. Your spirit guides were assigned to you by the highest power to help you along your physical path and physical journey. So, when you think of it logically, the very fact that you're from the light and your guides are from the light, there's absolutely nothing to be afraid of. In fact, there's no sane reason why you shouldn't be listening to your guides.

With that said, I've read a number of books and have heard other spiritual leaders discuss darkness and the dangers. Quite frankly, I'm not at all surprised why people are so frightened by that. But let me explain how your guides can help you eliminate that fear.

Picture a very sharp knife. It can be used carefully and safely to cut various foods. But it can also be unwisely used. You could cut yourself, or cut someone else. The knife itself is neither good nor bad. What matters is how you use it. It's the same with your guides. They are inherently safe. It's how you use them that matters. You don't need to fear the darkness. As many religious texts talk about, light always dispels darkness.

If you're in a dark room and can't see anything, you light a candle or a flashlight or flick on the lights to see. The light immediately destroys the darkness. That's what it's like with us. We don't need to worry about the evil and darkness because we dispel it through the light within us.

With all of that said, it never hurts to protect yourself with white light. It's almost like double protection to ensure that everything is good. Here is how to do that through a quick and simple meditation.

White Light Meditation

Close your eyes and imagine you're in a beautiful field.

There are beautiful rolling hills in every direction.

You're in the middle of nowhere, nobody can bother you, nobody can get to you.

Now just breathe.

Straight above you are the sky, clouds, and a beautiful white light coming through those clouds and shining down on you like a spotlight.

That bright white light is so bright, so warm. It feels like you're bathing in it, almost like standing in a shower with it flowing over you. It's an incredibly awesome feeling.

But you're not only surrounded in the white light...it flows inside you. It fills up every single molecule of you. You are flooded with that white light.

You can now choose for that white light to remain with you, or you can turn it off. I'm going to ask you to let it remain with you. I want you to say thank you. There you go. You're filled with white light. That light dispels the darkness.

Connecting with spirit is completely safe. By surrounding and filling yourself with white light, you've got added protection.

The rule of thumb is this: don't play with fire. I jokingly say in my live events to avoid evil like the plague. Don't 'conjure' up evil spirits and you'll be fine.

I had a discussion with a person recently about things like the Ouija board. Is the Ouija board dangerous? If you're walking down a street and you see a portal to hell, don't open it. I usually say that with a big smile in front of my audiences, and it gets a good laugh from them, because who in their right mind would open a portal to hell? But, if you use things like Ouija boards or anything else to conjure up the dark side, then that's your own doing. So, my advice is simple: don't do that. Fill yourself and surround yourself with white light. Connect with your spirit guides, and all shall be well.

Center Yourself: Following Your Breath

This one is my favorite, and one that I use on a daily basis. You don't need anything to do this. What I want you to do is breathe for a few moments. Breathe in through your nose and out through your mouth. It's as simple as that.

Unlike a lot of other meditative techniques that teach you to breathe in deeply and hold it, and then let it out with a sigh, you will not be doing that. You're just simply going to breathe, something that you've been doing since you were first born.

Imagine you can see your breath, like when it's cold outside. You can see it floating. Now imagine that you can see your breath going in through your nose, filling up your lungs, and exiting your mouth. See the breath go out.

This technique is called "Following Your Breath" because you are literally going to watch the breath go in through your nose. I want you to imagine you can see it filling your lungs up, and then when you naturally need to exhale, you just breathe it back out again.

Now imagine that you're sitting with other people. If the people beside you were just running, they're going to be breathing very, very quickly. You don't need to keep up with them. If you're breathing quickly, you don't have to focus on slowing your breath; you just have to concentration on breathing. Your body will naturally regulate it to the perfect state you need to be in. If the person beside you was breathing very, very slowly, you don't have to match his or her speed. Everyone has a unique pace of breathing in and out. Your job is simply to follow your breath.

You can do this with your eyes open, though I like to do this with my eyes closed. I would also like to point out that, if you were on a public bus or train going to work, for example, you could be sitting beside somebody and doing this meditation without that person even knowing what you're doing. There's no sign that you're actually doing the meditation. It's very cool.

As you do this breathing technique, you'll notice at some point that it will feel like a light is surrounding you and melting off the negative energies. It will feel like it's melting off the stresses. It will feel like it's burning away the things that are troubling you. You don't even need to think about that; it will just happen automatically for you.

What's also really cool about this technique is that you just follow your breath. If your mind is really busy and you're thinking about all kinds of other things, stuff that you have to do – maybe you have to pick up some groceries after work – don't let them distract you. Just acknowledge them and continue to follow your breath. You're not ignoring those other thoughts, you're just concentrating on your breath right now.

After about two minutes, you can stop and you'll discover that you'll feel much, much better. That's because you've only been focusing on your breath, which helps you naturally hit your base rhythm, which will allow you to connect with spirit. You will be centering yourself. It happens very quickly, and it only takes about two minutes to do. I use this one on a regular basis. It works tremendously well and is by far my favorite because you don't need to be anywhere special. You don't need to do anything unique. I use it multiple times a day, probably ten to fifteen times, maybe more. It's something that is easily used and easily acceptable.

Signs From Our Loved Ones

Can our loved ones send us signs from the afterlife?

They sure can!

Because our loved ones in spirit are no longer in physical form but are now energy, they have the ability to manipulate the environment around us.

Signs can come in all forms. You can receive signs through songs, feathers, light flickering, objects moving, etc. In fact, spirit is virtually unlimited in how they can present signs to us.

Unfortunately, there's a tremendous amount of misinformation on what signs are. In fact there have been books written that tell people how to decipher signs, causing people to suffer from paralysis by analysis.

If we are open to receiving signs, then our deceased loved ones will have no problem getting their messages delivered to us. However, in order for us to do that, we have to use a little bit of logic and common sense.

One of my neighbours a street over discovered I was a psychic medium. One day, when I was out for a walk, she stopped me to excitedly tell me that she had been receiving messages from her deceased husband.

"My husband puts feathers on my doorstep every day!" she said to me.

I didn't have the heart to tell her that there were pigeons roosting in an opening on the side of her house. Their flight path was over the front porch.

Not all signs are signs. While the feather could be a sign from a loved one, sometimes the feather is just a feather.

This chapter is going to help you understand the differences and to know, unequivocally, the signs when they come to you.

Bridges

One of the easiest ways to tell if a sign is actually a sign is with what my grandfather called a bridge.

Bridges come in two forms. The first is that whatever the sign is, it will instantly have a connection, or a bridge, to a memory.

For example, These can be dates, times, locations, or something that brings back an instant memory of an experience that you had with this loved one who is trying to get your attention.

An example would be finding a coin in an unusual spot and discovering that the year on the coin was the year of their passing. This would surely be a sign.

However, if you're standing at a bus stop and you find a coin on the ground, it is more likely than not that somebody simply dropped a coin. I would not consider that to be a sign.

See the difference? One stands out as unusual while the other is likely a normal occurrence.

Big difference.

The next type of bridge is more common. This is when a number of unique events occur over a short period of time but are linked with a common bridge.

Let me give you an example that just happened last week while I was working on this book.

I had run an errand on the other side of Phoenix, Arizona. When times are busy, I really enjoy going for nice long drives, and I was looking forward to this one-hour trip.

I hopped in my car and headed out. Just as I merged onto the highway, a wonderful memory of my dad popped into my head. He used to drive an 18-wheeler truck for a living. At that moment I thought it was just an association. You know, there are trucks on the highway... my dad drove a truck... a memory by association.

Regardless, I smiled and just kept on driving.

I was driving in the fast lane when I noticed in my rear view mirror a blue Cadillac coming up quickly behind me. I changed lanes to let them pass. As they zipped by, I noticed a bumper sticker on the Caddy. It was the Scottish flag.

I couldn't believe my eyes. Even though I'm a psychic medium and I do this for a living, sometimes the signs just blow me away. My dad was born in Aberdeen, Scotland. I was fiercely proud of his heritage.

I chuckled to myself and said out loud, "Hi, Dad!"

If that wasn't enough, what would happen to me next clearly proved to me that this wasn't a coincidence...

I turned on the radio in my car and the AC/DC song "It's a Long Way to the Top" was playing!

If you're not familiar with the song, it's unique because half of it features bagpipes playing over the driving rhythm. My dad hated hard rock, but when I was younger, I forced him to listen to the song. He immediately didn't like it, but as soon as the bagpipes started playing, he literally changed his tune. No pun intended. He thought the bagpipes were fantastic!

I must have looked like a maniac driver as I was laughing my head off and singing at the top my lungs out of pure joy and bliss that my dad had come to say hello.

Can you see the bridges? Independently, the events could have been coincidences. For example, I have listened to that AC/DC song many times without thinking about my father. And, of course, it's not the first car I've ever seen with a bumper sticker of Scotland. That alone would not make me think it's a sign from my father.

But the bridge of all three happening in rapid succession certainly convinced me it was a message.

Signs: Blair's Five Rules

Years ago, when I used to teach psychic development classes, I came up with Blair's five rules of signs. Everyone seemed to enjoy them, and they helped give some clarity on the differences between real signs versus just coincidences.

You don't need to memorize them. Just read through them and get a clear understanding. I know they will help you.

Rule number one: There are no rules when it comes to spirit signs.

When I used to share that with the students, it would often get a laugh. But it's the truth.

Think about it. When you leave your physical body, you'll become energy. Spirit – your soul – is energy because you'll easily be able to manipulate the things around you. Isn't that fun?

Rule number two: Signs come when you least expect them.

Because our loved ones are in spirit, they know better than we do when the right time is to make a connection.

Signs don't come to us out of desperation; we must be at peace first to best receive them.

Consider this: your loved ones will always show you signs when it is of the helping nature; it will never be at a time when it could hurt you.

That's why there's usually a little bit of time from when the person passes to the first connection or sign. Our loved ones wish to give us the space and time to mourn and process the physical death.

This is especially true if the death is tragic. Typically, those of us left behind are in utter shock and disbelief when this occurs. Our loved ones often will leave us the space to process the shock and adjust to the passing before they will ever show us a sign.

And that makes sense doesn't it? How cruel would it be for them to start showing signs at that particular point? It would be like adding gas to a fire and making grief worse.

Of course, there are always exceptions to the rule. A friend of ours lost her husband in Iraq, and he came to her through connection while she was sleeping to say goodbye. It braced her for the news that she would receive officially from the military.

But the most important thing to keep in mind is to avoid comparisons. In the case of our friend, her husband came through for a particular reason. Most the time they give us a grieving period in which to mourn.

Rule number three: If there is a doubt, throw it out!

That's a catchy one, isn't it?

Please discount any obvious signs. I've already shared some examples, such as the lady who had the pigeons roosting, pennies in common areas, light bulbs flickering because they're about to burn out, etc.

Remember that there will always be a bridge when there is a sign from a deceased loved one. An obvious connection.

I'm not asking you to be skeptical, but I am asking you to use some common sense. Just like the old adage "Don't believe everything you see and hear," the same applies here.

Let there be no doubt: when you are open to the signs, your loved ones will be loud and clear.

Rule number four: Signs often come in threes.

Notice that I said "often." They can come in the form of single signs, but more often than not, when loved ones are trying to reach us, they will give us multiple signs to experience. And just like my dad coming to visit me in the car on my mini road trip, You'll likely discover your loved ones will give you signs in threes as well.

It's worth noting that first the signs may be unrelated. But upon reflection, they will all link together thanks to those bridges.

Many people discover that it's kind of like doing a puzzle. The individual pieces may not make sense at the moment, but when you piece them all together, the picture comes together.

It's the same here. You won't need to stretch to make something fit; it will fit naturally. Remember rule number three? If you're in doubt, it's likely not a sign.

Let's say you're looking back on your day and you're sure that three incidents were definitely signs, but you're not sure about the fourth. Then toss out the fourth. It's that simple.

Here's another reason why you should do that: it demonstrates to spirit that you're not grasping at straws and that you're open to receiving signs. This is not a negative thing. In fact, it's one of the most positive things you can do. Don't believe everything that you see and hear. Don't allow yourself to become gullible. Instead, seek clarity from your loved ones.

Rule number five: Don't be afraid to ask for clarity.

There's a major difference between being unsure of the sign versus demanding that you're deceased loved ones prove themselves.

Here's what I mean. While you shouldn't demand that your loved ones show you specific signs on specific dates or at specific times, there's absolutely nothing wrong with asking them to clarify something.

I do this all time. When I'm giving my mediumship demonstrations and I'm connecting with a deceased loved one, they'll sometimes show me signs or tell me things that I just don't understand. So I simply ask them to clarify.

Does that make sense? It's perfectly okay to say to somebody "I don't know what you mean – could you please clarify?" And you're welcome to do it here. Just make sure you're doing it through a respectful and honest heart.

Let's say you find a coin in your house but it's close to the laundry basket. You weren't sure if this is a message from your loved one because it's in a rather obvious place. Simply smile and say "I love you, and if this is you, please show me another sign."

Don't make a big thing about signs

Please understand that while signs are a terrific way for loved ones to show us that they are still around and that they are still okay, Don't set yourself up for disappointment by demanding signs on a regular basis.

Doing so will only cause you more grief. And that's counter to what they want for you!

Know this: your loved ones are okay. They are around and watching you. But they also want you to become independent and move forward and live the remainder of your life fully.

I like to think of signs as postcards from the other side. When I was little boy, I had an aunt who traveled a lot. She would send postcards from wherever she visited. She didn't write much, as her handwriting was large, but she'd almost always finish off by saying "Thinking of you with love."

Signs are just like those postcards. You are meant to get them every single day, but you will only get them from time to time, and often when you least expect them. Embrace them for what they are: kind words from the other side, proving that love never dies.

Tips: Opening the door to receive signs

Is there a way to open the door, so to speak, to the other side? Yes, there is, and I will share those tips with you right now.

The recurring theme here is that we often live such busy lives that we miss the small subtle signs from our loved ones. It's my hope that by the end of this book I'll have driven that home effectively!

Meditation

My first tip is to practice the breathing meditation I shared with you earlier. It allows you to clear your mind and focus on becoming one with spirit. The breathing meditation will help you become more aware of your surroundings, yourself, and any signs that may be shown.

The meditation alone will help you greatly in becoming more aware of the signs. I meditate multiple times each day. At the very least, I meditate in the morning and before I go to bed.

As simple as that may sound, it works wonders. Meditate.

Affirmation/Prayer

A simple affirmation/prayer helps. You only need to do this once. Don't make the mistake of doing this repeatedly as it's annoying to spirit!

Here's a terrific simple affirmation: "I love you, I miss you, and I am ready to receive any sign when you are ready."

Isn't that lovely? It works well, particularly if you let go of any demand for a timeframe. Try it.

Discard Preconceived Definitions

This is a big one: you do NOT need books that tell you the 'meanings' of signs.

At every live event I do, I get someone who will ask me something along the lines of, "What does seeing a dove (or fill in the blank) mean?"

The truth is that it's not the symbol that counts, it's the message behind it. And the message can be different for different people.

When I do mediumship connections, if a deceased loved one shows me white roses, it means for me to say "I love you" to the person being read. However, when another famous television medium sees white roses, that means for him to say "Happy birthday" or to mention a celebration. And to yet another medium it means they are to let the person know the spirit is happy and good on the other side.

Same white rose, completely different meanings.

Let go of the meanings. Embrace the signs. A sign, like that postcard, is just the way for spirit to send love to you and let you know they haven't gone away.

The beauty of becoming spiritual and connecting with spirit is that it transcends logic. Spirit is beyond thinking. When a message comes through, you'll know what the message is. It can be as simple as an "I love you," or a concern they have for you.

You'll know.

For the sake of completeness, I am including a list of the most common signs people get and what they can mean. But don't get hung up on those. Read them and then move on to the next chapter.

Common Signs

Smells and fragrances

Scents and fragrances are a very common way for our loved ones to let us know they are near.

The scent will almost always be unique or unusual. If you wear the same perfume as your mother, then that scent should be discounted. However, if you don't wear it and don't have it in your home and you suddenly catch a whiff of it... guess who is saying hello?

Touches

Touches can come in many forms. A feeling of having hair brushed from your forehead, to a hand on your shoulder, to being rubbed up against by your deceased and beloved cat.

Speaking of pets, many people have reported that their beds feel warm where their cat or dog used to lay.

Or the feeling of a spouse hogging the bed like they did while alive.

Feeling Their Presence

A very common sign is the feeling that you are not alone, as though your loved one is in the room with you. It's a comforting feeling. Typically this feeling will be felt in shared common areas like the living room where you watched television together, the kitchen, bedroom, etc.

I recently spoke to a client who has an old-fashioned porch with a swing on it. She would swing while her husband would rock in his rocking chair. She feels him routinely when on the porch. She says she "knows" he's there... and he is!

Songs And Music

Our loved ones are able to spark off fabulous memories with music. It is not necessarily 'your' song either. Obscure songs that you may not even like can often bring back a flood of wonderful memories of a long-forgotten time or event.

Many years ago my friend's mother took a trip overseas. When she came back, we had a surprise party for her. My friend, a real character, played Elton John's

"Bitch Is Back" and got a big laugh. I was very close to his mom, and when I heard that on the radio one day, I immediately was flooded with wonderful memories of that hilarious event and other things we'd gotten in trouble for. Guess who was visiting and saying "hello?"

Shadows

Not the scary shadows like in horror movies. No bogeymen coming after you!

I'm talking about the shadows that appear out of the corner of your eye, or in a hallway in the absence of a light source that could cause it.

While it might seem obvious when pointed out, tall shadows are going to be people, whereas smaller ones are likely pets on the other side.

Clouds and Shapes

When you see a meaningful shape in a cloud, it is literally a 'sign from above.'

Please remember that if you have to stare and really use your imagination to 'make' a shape, it's not a sign. Always remember – there will be bridges that will make the image meaningful and validated.

Visions In Mirrors Or Reflective Objects

My granda said that mirrors can be a portal to the other side, and I believe this to be true. I believe reflective surfaces (not just mirrors) have the ability at times to almost 'see' the other side, if only briefly.

I'm not talking about scrying, which is a divination practice of looking into a crystal ball or a special mirror. That's different.

We're talking about looking into a mirror and briefly seeing faces, shapes, or signs that are linked to our loved ones on the other side. This phenomenon can happen looking into still water at a lake, for instance, or a glass window that is reflecting light.

Otherworld Thoughts

When a thought pops into your head that you know is not yours, this can often be attributed to either your spirit guides or a deceased loved one. While I don't like the use of the word telepathic to describe this, that's very much what it is... it's your loved ones delivering a message.

Typically you'll know it is because it will be 'said' in a manner or way you wouldn't be likely to use.

An example: I was in my garage and I looked at a shelf that had some garden tools. I immediately thought, "That looks queer," which was an expression my father used to use when something he was building didn't look level or quite right. It used to drive me nuts as I told him that it was a derogatory term for homosexuals. He rightly informed me that while that may be one definition, it also meant something wasn't level or right, which is the actual definition.

I didn't pay attention, and the next day we heard a big crash. We discovered the shelf wasn't installed properly and fell to the floor with all the tools. What would have been an easy fix ended up being a big mess.

Guess who warned me?

Pets Seeing Things

This is cool. Pets, particularly dogs and cats, are able to pick up on spirits moving in houses. I'm not talking about a dog watching a fluff or fly zipping around. I'm talking about the uncanny experience of watching your pet 'follow' something around.

A good friend of mine lives in an old home. Every night at the same time, his dog Brutus gets up from the foot of the bed, looks up, and cautiously follow 'someone' down the hall to the kitchen. Every night.

Rainbows

Rainbows can be a sign from a loved one on two conditions: the rainbow should be a surprise (or at least unexpected) and there needs to be a bridge to the loved one in some manner.

The problem with rainbows, in my opinion, is that they are common after rain and then sudden sunlight. Sometimes a rainbow is just... a rainbow. Honor the validations that come by appreciating the signs that are signs and enjoying the rainbows that are a natural phenomenon. You will know the difference. Without trying.

Butterflies

I love butterflies. Always have. A butterfly landing on or very near you is almost always a sign from your loved ones in spirit. Butterflies represent a true transformation, as they essentially cocoon in order to transition from caterpillar to butterfly.

Butterflies always serve as reminders to me to stop and meditate any time I see them, because to my mind they are a reminder that spirit exists and that our loved ones never die.

Feathers

Feathers have a powerful and meaningful connection to the spirit world. North American Indian Chiefs wear feathers in their headdresses to represent communication with the other side. Feathers as messages from spirit are common among many religions and faiths.

The generally accepted meaning is that of encouragement. If you are planning a job change and you find a feather, it can mean encouragement from beyond.

With that said, I encourage you to be open to the bridge you will have along with the message. It will become clear to you without effort or 'definition.'

Candles Flickering

This is a bit bizarre and hilarious at the same time! Candles will sometimes flicker wildly in the absence of a draft/breeze.

We had a candle that my grandmother gave us. After she died, we lit it from time to time. One time it started flickering like crazy and my dad said, "That's Nani waving 'hello' to us." I laughed hysterically at that until I later realized this is a common way for spirit to connect with us.

Pennies From Heaven

Coins can be a way for spirit to grab our attention. However, I can absolutely assure you that there is no coin mint in heaven and they aren't throwing them from the sky.

A coin message must always be in an unusual place that a coin wouldn't be in normally. There will always be a bridge as well in the form of 'knowing' who it's from - the date on the coin or something to do with the object or location of the coin.

Dragonflies

Dragonflies hold several meanings. Like the butterfly they represent transformation, but their flittering and flightiness is a reminder to slow down. Their colors change depending on the light and angle and remind us to step back and understand that things aren't always as they seem.

To be clear: dragonflies are not 'bad omens' or negative in any way. Just like a stop sign, they are there to remind us to stop, take a good look around, and evaluate a situation. This is good, not bad.

Hummingbird

A hummingbird represents many things: uniqueness (they can hover and fly backwards), strength, a joy of life, dedication, and boldness.

Hummingbirds that behave in an unusual manner, such as flying into a house to look around and then leave, is a sure sign from loved ones that you are being checked upon.

Numbers

In the past few years, too much weight has been put on numbers. Numbers will always have a bridge that will highlight a meaningful connection to a loved one.

Please don't put too much weight on times such as 11:11 as it could literally mean you happened to look at the clock at... 11:11. When the numbers hit, they will hit hard and in a meaningful way.

Pictures: falling or tilting

This is a cool phenomenon! A photo of a loved one falls or tilts in an unusual manner. It's marked because all of the other photos nearby will be in perfect order. It's a sure sign the loved one is trying to get your attention.

A client in New Zealand told me of the reverse happening. She felt her dad's presence for days and felt he was telling her she'd be alright. But, alright from what? A few days later, a massive tremor hit. Although the entire house was shaken, walls were cracked, dishes were broken, etc., all of the photos on the wall fell except one. The picture that remained was her dad, and it was hanging perfectly.

Electrical Items Behaving Strangely

Lights flickering. Televisions and radios turning on and off. Kitchen appliances turning on by themselves.

These are almost always caused by loved ones who are "troublemakers." They aren't trying to scare you, but in almost every case they are the pranksters of the spirit world.

Phone Messages

This is a relatively new phenomenon. A voice mail message from beyond. Sometimes with speaking, but most often from the number of the deceased showing up on your call display.

This phenomenon is also done via text messages and email.

Clocks Stopping

There are two different phenomena. Sometimes upon the death of someone a clock will suddenly stop at the exact time of death. In other words, the clock 'dies' when the person dies.

The other phenomenon is a watch winding down and stopping at a significant time to the deceased/yourself.

I recently found an old watch, the one that I would have worn when my father died. The time on the watch? Seven o'clock. My father's time of death? Seven o'clock in the morning. The watch needed a new battery, but was this a coincidence? I think not.

Sleep Connections

The easiest and most common way for deceased loved ones to make connections with us is while we are sleeping.

Whenever I ask at a live event how many people have experienced a loved one coming to them during their dreams, almost the entire audience raise their hands or nods their heads.

When our deceased loved ones come to us, they're often happy, healthy, and completely at peace. Many people are shocked to see their loved one come to them in that form.

It's human nature to remember our loved one as we last remember them. We often remember how sick they were, remember them suffering on their deathbed and in pain. So when they do come to us happy, alive, and vibrant, it's a bit of shock. And for many people, this can cause us to doubt what we just dreamed.

This is natural, but by the end of this chapter you'll know the difference between a dream and a visitation. You'll learn to embrace these wonderful and beautiful spirit connections!

Not only that, I'm going to show you how you can help facilitate a connection.

Why is sleep the most common way for our loved ones to connect?

When you're asleep your critical mind, or your conscious mind, is completely shutdown. You aren't thinking, processing, analyzing, or doing anything except getting the rest and rejuvenation that your body needs. And because of this your guard is let down, so to speak. Because of this it allows your loved ones to be able to easily access you through direct messaging.

When you're sleeping you are no longer consciously or subconsciously blocking the messages from spirit.

Of course, when you wake up, so does your critical mind. This often leads to doubt that the connections you had while you were asleep were real.

Not long ago I was doing a live demonstration of mediumship. During my question and answer segment, a lady asked me about dreams and the connections that she was having. Suddenly, my guides gave me an amazing revelation of the difference between dreams and connections.

You Do Not Connect With Loved Ones During Dreams

Up until this event, like most psychics and mediums, I used to erroneously tell people that our loved ones came to us in our dreams. This is not correct.

Right in the middle of my demonstration, while I was answering this lady's question, my guides corrected me in midsentence. Our loved ones do not connect with us during our dreams. They connect with us while we are asleep.

As soon as this was revealed to me, I had one of those amazing aha moments. Understanding the difference between a dream and a spirit connection is easy once you grasp this. It'll answer almost all the questions and objections that you may have about the connections that you receive.

Let's talk about dreams first. Dreams are weird. Dreams often make no sense whatsoever.

You'll wake up in the morning, for example, and re- member dreaming that you were going to work in the morning. You got up, got dressed, and jumped on a giant rubber ducky. The big giant yellow rubber ducky. And instead of driving down the road, you actually floated down the stream on that rubber ducky. On the side of the stream were circus clowns waving at you with balloons.

You wake up in the morning and say to yourself, "What the heck?"

That was a dream. Dreams are nonsensical and meaningless.

Another common feature of dreams is that when you wake up, you'll only remember parts of the dream.

For example you may remember that you were speaking to the postman. However, the post man was faceless. And by faceless, I don't mean a scary faceless person; I mean a person who you can't remember the details of.

In some dreams you will have friends and loved ones who participate in the dream, but they often don't have any specific or logical role. They were just there, so to speak.

Dreaming and sleep are very important to our personal health and well-being. Dreaming is completely normal, but that is not the way our loved ones on the other side make connections with us.

Our loved ones make connections with us while we are sleeping, either before or after we've achieved the dream state. It's really important to understand the difference. Once you get the difference, it'll really open up the connections from your loved ones for you. And that's exciting, isn't it?

Spirit connections while we are sleeping are very real and vivid. Unlike the example of the faceless person I mentioned above, the loved ones will come through to us as clear as day. You will clearly see them. You will clearly know that's them. You will clearly recognize details of them.

They will be real, clear, and vivid. You will not wake up having any doubt of whom you saw or whom you connected with.

Rule Number One: Connections will be clear. Key word: clear.

Isn't that exciting?

Here's my personal rule of thumb: if you wake up in the morning and what you experienced while sleeping was weird, strange, or unclear, dismiss it. Smile and just simply know that you had a terrific dream and nothing more.

But if you wake up in the morning knowing that you had a clear, precise connection, rejoice! Your loved one has just made a connection with you. You had contact with the other side.

At this point, I like to remind you that all messages from spirit will always be positive. Although you might not like the message they deliver, it will always be for your highest good.

Our spirit guides guide us and our loved ones love us. Our loved ones in spirit will always support us, although maybe not in the way we wish they would.

Let me give you an example. I live in the United States. I'm a Canadian. My background is Scottish and I love beer.

I moved down to Phoenix, Arizona, in the United States a number of years ago, and I discovered the beer here is inexpensive. In fact, if you buy beer on sale, it's as cheap as pop is in Canada.

I've never been a fan of pop, so I started stocking up on beer. Of course during the summertime it gets hot in Arizona. After all, it is the desert! So around one o'clock in the afternoon on a hot day, I would find myself popping open a can of light beer. Of course, around three o'clock it would get even hotter and, being Thursday, I'd have another beer. And so on.

Now I'd like to point out that I've long given up getting drunk for fun. I don't drink to get drunk. I just like beer!

But like most bad habits, this one sneaked up on me and became a regular occurrence. I was drinking beer every single day, and a fair amount of it. My waistline was proof!

Deep down inside I knew I was drinking too much booze. And while I can argue that I didn't drink to get drunk, the amount of alcohol I was drinking was not a healthy amount.

One night our 'low battery' alert on our fire alarm kept going off. It kept me awake half the night until I finally got up and fixed it. Naturally, around noon, I was dead tired and decided to go for a nap. I fell deep asleep and, while sleeping, my dad came to me in a spirit connection.

There was no mistaking him. It was Dad clear as day. The details were vivid. Let me explain.

In the late 1950s my mother knitted a beautiful jacket for my father. It was light blue, and on the back was a giant fish caught in the fisherman's hook splashing out of the water. It was my dad's favorite spring and fall jacket.

He wore that sweater so much, but there were no elbows to the jacket, the shoulders frayed, and there were holes all over.

One day I came home and found my dad was livid. He rarely got angry and rarely raised his voice. But my mother got fed up with the jacket and ended up tossing it out without asking my dad first. It's funny to think of it now, but for some reason that jacket is in my memory forever.

In the connection that I had with my dad he was wearing that exact jacket, holes and all. He had a big smile and was holding a bottle of beer. The beer was a cream ale beer that I got my dad hooked on just before he passed away. He loved it.

Without saying a single word, I knew exactly the message my dad was delivering to me. I knew he was concerned with the amount of alcohol I was consuming and I knew that I had to cut back.

More importantly, I felt a tremendous amount of love from my dad. I didn't feel he was judging me, nor did I feel like he was putting me down. All I felt was that love and concern for my health and my personal well-being.

When I awoke, I knew that I had to start cutting back. I knew the message wasn't to quit drinking. It was to start drinking moderately.

Of course I was quite emotional when I woke up because it felt like he was just there. I felt like if I had only opened my eyes a split second earlier, he would've been standing by the couch where I was snoozing.

What did I do? Well, as hard as it was to admit it to myself, I knew I was drinking too much and I immediately cut back how much I was having each day. I still drink beer, of course, but not as much as I used to. And I'm sure my liver and my body are happier because that!

Rule Number Two: Messages will always be for your highest good. You might not like the message, and that's okay. But whatever it is, it will be to help you, not hinder you.

Many people worry that spirit connections with their loved ones will be scary in some way, shape, or form. Let me assure you that the connections are not scary in any way.

Because our loved ones are only going to connect with us to share love and support, they're not going to do anything to scare us.

Our loved ones in spirit are going to give us reassurance, encouragement, and confidence.

Connections can be overwhelmingly emotional. There's no getting around that. In the example above I was very emotional, but my father came through and connected with me. But it wasn't scary in any way.

One of my clients recently shared with me that her husband came to her only a couple of nights after he had passed. He was in a terrible accident and had to have his legs amputated. He was in intensive care for about a week before he succumbed to his injuries.

She was sleeping and she remembers him coming in to tuck her into bed. He worked late, was a night owl, and often tucked her in when he would come home. When she saw him in the visitation she was startled that he was back to full health. He had his legs, looked happy, and she could hear him say as clear as day, "Love you, honey."

She doubted the connection. She said to me, "Blair, he had legs."

"Of course he had legs," I said to her. "He was coming to let you know that he was back to perfect health in spirit and no longer suffering and in pain. He was also coming to let you know how much he really loved you."

She exploded into tears. Not painful tears, but tears of joy. It took a long time for her to get her composure back, but she thanked me for my help in understanding. He wanted her to remember him in perfect health, not as she last saw him. He wanted her to know that although he was gone, he would always love her.

She was relieved and felt a tremendous weight lifted off of her shoulders.

The two examples above show the different ways that our loved ones can communicate with us. In the example with my father, he said absolutely nothing to me. I realized and understood through symbolism exactly the message he wanted to communicate.

It's difficult to put into words exactly how I "know" this, But that's the nature of these types of connections. We are not talking logic here. We're talking about a special spiritual communication. I don't need to prove to anybody what the message was, I knew what the message was. It will be the same for you. You'll know.

In the example of my client who lost her husband, her over-analytical mind could have discounted any connection with her husband. Thankfully, though, she asked me for my input, and when she dropped the overthinking and just accepted the message, it became very clear.

Sometimes our loved ones will come to us with no specific message. Other times they will come with a very specific message for us. No matter what kind of message you get, know this: love never dies, and your loved ones are always near.

The Spirit Connection Experience

Would you like to experience a connection with a loved one tonight?

I'm betting you just said yes, didn't you?

Several times a year I facilitate a worldwide event that I call the Blair Robertson Spirit Connection Experience. They are quite popular and often have thousands of participants. (You should sign up for my free weekly email and get in on these and other seminars, books, and tour dates.)

On a specific date and time, thousands of people literally work together in concert to ask spirit to help facilitate a connection with a loved one on the other side. It works incredibly well. While it takes a lot of effort on my end to conduct these events, the stories that I hear afterward are very rewarding. I'll share a couple of stories shortly.

The Secret

The secret to the success of these massive Spirit Connection Experiences is this: to ask for a connection not for yourself, but to earnestly pray that a connection happens to everyone else instead.

By praying for a connection for others, we enter into a spiritual space of selflessness and love, which spirit responds to best.

"How does that help me?" you may ask. Great question! Consider this: when you are praying for a connection for thousands of others on a specific night... you have thousands of people praying for YOU, don't you?

It works, and it's profound when it does. I do them about three times a year. I encourage you to get my newsletter to join in on the next one. There's no cost.

www.BlairRobertson.com

In the meantime, here's something you can try. It's a wonderful spirit ceremony that was passed down to me by my grandfather.

The Spirit Connection Ceremony

This lovely little ceremony is surprisingly easy. It's safe, practical, and fun to do. And the best part is that I can tell you, from personal experience, that thousands have had success with it.

With that said, you must follow these simple rules and have faith.

Here's what you'll need:

1. A very small piece of paper and a pen.

2. A memento of a loved one you want to make a spirit connection with. Don't make this step hard, okay? A simple photo, maybe a war medal, a favorite pipe, Mom's favorite vase... it makes no difference, as long as there is a "connection" between the object, you, and your loved one.

3. Have a white candle alongside the photo/memento. Natural beeswax is best. Natural beeswax is cream, not

white. However, don't be concerned if you don't have it. A plain white one will do. Do the best you can with what you have.

4. Pick a night in the very near future to try this. We call this an intention, and once a date is set, your spirit guides will be 'on alert,' so to speak.

A few guidelines before we start.

It's important that you do not abuse this ceremony. It is meant for special occasions and not to be used 'regularly.' If you are tempted to try this every night, it will surely not work.

Now, while it is best to do during a special occasion such as Christmas, anniversaries (such as weddings), dates of death, etc., you most certainly can do this at any other time. So, feel free to try this out in the next day or so. In fact, I encourage you to do so! I wouldn't do it tonight if you are reading this book for the first time. I'd suggest tomorrow night at the earliest.

Here's the ceremony as I have done it many times.

I like to have my candle, memento, and paper on my night stand. With that said, my mom would use the fireplace mantle and, once completed, go immediately to bed.

Get yourself ready for bed. You want this ceremony to be the very last thing you do before you go to sleep.

I personally begin by asking for white light protection, as discussed earlier in this and all of my books.

Light the white candle. Write the name of the loved one you are wishing to make a connection with on the piece of paper and fold it twice.

I like to put my hand on the memento or hold the picture and think back to a happy memory of them. Please do not dredge up negative memories, regrets, or how they passed or suffered.

Now, ask your spirit guides to assist you in making a connection while you sleep. Again, keep it simple; you don't need to beg or plead. Just a simple request that's short and sweet: "I would love to make a connection with (name) in spirit tonight. Thank you."

If you can safely do so, you can burn the paper with the name on it. Please be careful in doing so and make sure that the ashes are completely out. Alternately - and this works just as well - you can simply tear the paper twice. No matter what you choose, the paper with the name must be destroyed as you are ceremoniously letting the person go free in spirit. This is very important; don't skip this.

Blow out the candle. Again, please make sure it's completely extinguished. And for goodness sake, do not let it burn unattended all night.

Hop into bed, say your loved one's name once, and then go to sleep.

See how easy that is?

If you follow this ceremony, the odds are extraordinarily high that you will have a connection while you sleep.

Do not set expectations. Connections come in all forms, so be completely open to whatever comes.

The connection you have may be as simple as a brief appearance, or a loved one may bring a message. No matter what, the underlying message will be of love and you'll know they are near.

Some see their loved ones. Some hear them. Others feel them or 'know' that they were near. Some have a feeling of being 'watched over' while sleeping. Connections come in all shapes and sizes.

When you awaken, one of two things will occur (sometimes both). One is that you will have a very strong sensation that someone was 'just there.' Not in a scary way, mind you. So if you live alone, don't worry. You won't be scared. But it will feel like someone was just standing at your bed... and here's the key part... it will feel like if you had just opened your eyes a split second before, you would have caught them. You can't, of course, but that's the feeling.

The other thing you will notice is a tremendous feeling of peace. Many, many people report that they have one of the best night's sleep in recent memory.

See, when you have a connection while you are sleeping, it brings with it an overwhelming feeling of peace and love.

And it gets better. If you allow yourself to become aware of the signs that are around you as we discussed in another chapter, you'll likely discover - as many do - that the signs will continue throughout the next day.

Give it a try soon, and do it on special occasions. I wish for you many happy connections.

Successes

Here are a few testimonies from a Spirit Connection Experience I conducted in late 2014. Note the various types of connections, yet the theme 'love never dies' runs through them all.

"It all started in my dream on this Boxing Day morning. I was in my old neighbourhood, where I hadn't been since I was in my early 30s. The place doesn't even exist anymore. We were parking the car in the driveway when I looked up toward our living room window, which resembled much of what my current living room window looks like now. There stood my dad and my stepmother waving hello and smiling at me. They were both so happy to see me. My dad was wearing the Christmas suit we bought him as a Christmas gift and that he was buried in. My stepmother looked like she was wearing a dress, but she had a kerchief in her hair as if she was getting ready. They waved and smiled at me for what felt like two minutes. She then looked up at my dad as if to say, 'Why are we still waving?' But my dad just kept on waving. I came in and he asked what we were doing there. I told him that I had taken over their place and was fixing it up (which is what we are doing with the new house we bought and not their old place). You could feel a sense of happiness and joy around them. They were soooooo happy to have been able to make that connection, as was

I. On Boxing Day, my dad and stepmom would go visit her side of the family, so I guess they were getting ready to go visit the family today. Thank you, Blair, for opening the door to allow for this wonderful experience. It's been eight years since he passed and three years since she passed. All the best to everyone who was able to experience something so wonderful. Happy holidays to you all." Monique

"When I went to bed Christmas Eve, it was actually already Christmas Day at 12:30 A.M. Just before going to sleep, I felt a hand touching the side of my head. I have had this experience before, so I know that somebody was around - and I have been told by another medium that it is my mother. Please keep up your good work. We may not tell you how much we appreciate you, but rest assured we do. Compliments of the season to you and your family." Kenneth

"On Christmas Day at about noon, my husband and I were relaxing in the sun (we were on holiday in Mexico), and all of a sudden the clearest vision came to me. It was my husband and me hugging and holding a beautiful little blonde girl (I am pregnant with a little girl). We were kissing her and laughing, and kissing each other, too. Right beside us in the vision I could see Chris's mother. She was young and beautiful, and she was with a boy – Chris's brother. Both have passed on (I didn't write his name because I could only put one – I put

Chris's mother, Sue). Chris's mother and brother both had their arms wrapped around the three of us as we kissed and hugged our little girl and each other, but we couldn't seem to see them....they just seemed to be there protecting us. It was so real, and so beautiful. Thank you, Blair. xoxox TL

"Dear Blair, I followed all your steps. That night I went to bed and my daughter was sleeping next to me. In the middle of the night my daughter sat up and said that Peter was just in the room. Peter is my son who died in February of this year. She was so excited (in the morning she didn't remember this happening). I also went to my sister's house and she couldn't find her gravy bowl. It was my grandma's (also deceased), but it wasn't in its spot. My sister just happened to find it in a spot where she knows she didn't put it, and inside was the flower my son made her when he was in preschool. Mind you, he had just turned nineteen when he died. There were a lot of signs that day, but these were the most important. Thank you and bless you. Love and light." Jill

"Blair, I have to say I was a little bit skeptical, but very hopeful. I burned my candle all Christmas Eve next to a picture of my mom. During the evening the candle highlighted my mom's picture. I dismissed it because it would have just highlighted the way it was sitting next to the candle. The next morning I awoke and heard my teenage daughters laughing and giggling and singing

Christmas songs at the top of their lungs trying to wake us. I came into the family room and they had breakfast prepared - and to my surprise, they had lit the candle next to my mom's picture.

"They did not know why it was there; I hadn't told anyone what I was doing. They had never lit candles before. We all started with the unwrapping of presents. The last one given to me was a cameo on a necklace. My mom's favourite necklace was a cameo on a ribbon. I know that she had a guiding hand in choosing that necklace. Thank you, Blair. It was the first time in thirty-three years that I know my mom is here with me."

Tina

T.A.L.K. To Your Deceased Loved Ones

"Just TALK to them!"

Sylvia Browne

I've saved the best for last. This is a technique I have shared with countless people in my live seminars going back to the 1990s.

My dad called the technique "Going Into The Silence" because that's exactly what you will be doing. I call it T.A.L.K. to help remember the steps needed. The best part? It's easy to do.

What does going into the silence mean? Let me give you an example. We used to have an old clock at our cottage that literally ticked rhythmically.

In the daytime, you could hear all the wildlife, neighbours outdoors, boats in the distance, Mom's radio shows playing quietly.

But at night, tucked in bed, the world went silent. The wildlife was sleeping, all the neighbours were sound asleep. Everything and everyone was dead quiet. Except... tick, tick, tick.

Going into the silence allows us to hear what is normally drowned out. Going into the silence, in this case, means going into the spirit realm and having a conversation with a loved one!

Isn't that exciting?

The only problem with what I am about to teach you is that it is often met with skepticism at first because it is so simple and effective.

That, and you'll likely feel a wee bit silly your first time doing it. You will likely question the process.

I'm about to teach you exactly how to have a T.A.L.K. with your deceased loved ones!

Not only that, your loved ones in spirit will provide you with validations that it really is them.

Preparation

Preparation for this is easy. In fact, I urge you to keep it simple and basic.

If possible, I want you to go to a place that was favoured by the person with whom you are wishing to connect.

It might be their favourite chair, room, an outside deck, a garden, a tree, the car in the garage...

When my dad was alive, we'd often have 'chats.' Nine times out of ten they were in the kitchen of his house (and later in his apartment).

Dad had this crappy kitchen table with metal legs and an ugly mustard top. The chairs were cushioned plastic and matched the table. The chairs were comfortable and I'd sit while he brewed and served the tea.

I can still see him across the table as we chatted.

What if these places no longer exist?

Well, in my case, my dad's apartment and furniture are long gone. So, in this case, go to a place where you believe they would likely gravitate to if they were still alive.

For example, I just know that my dad would love our little bar area and stools. He wasn't much of a drinker at all, but loved cozy little spots to sit and chat. That would be it if he were here today. I'm certain of it.

It also helps to have something personal of theirs. It could be a ring, necklace, photo - any memento that belonged to them.

I believe that having something of theirs helps us feel closer to them. But again, if you don't have anything, don't worry.

Go Into The Silence

Here's what you do: go to the place your loved one enjoyed and feel free to sit in their favourite spot. Maybe it's a rocking chair. Or, go to a place you know they'd enjoy.

Begin your mindful meditation to become one with spirit and to quiet your mind. Do this for a few minutes until your mind goes quiet. Don't rush. Everyone is different, so just keep breathing until you get to that perfect state.

Now, here's the fun part... start t.a.l.k.ing to them!

And when I say fun, I mean it. Chatter away!

T.A.L.K. stands for:

T: Talk to them. Chatter away as though they were literally there in front of you.

A: Ask them questions. I'll illustrate this in detail shortly, but when you talk with someone, don't you ask the other person questions? Of course. And you'll do the same here.

L: Listen to them. Your loved ones will give you feedback.

K: Know that it really is your loved one by getting confirmations through signs.

I watched the late Sylvia Browne being interviewed on television one night. She was known for being direct and blunt. Sylvia was asked, "How do you connect with your loved ones in spirit?" and she replied, "Just TALK to them!"

Ain't gonna get plainer than that!

When I would do this with groups, I would encourage everyone to do it silently. But in your own private conversation, feel free to talk out loud.

TALK:

Start off with their name and tell them whatever is on your mind. "Hey Mom! Guess what? Little Suzie graduated top of her class... and you know your favourite plant that you loved so much? Well, I overwatered it and now it's dead... I told you I had a black thumb... I miss you and was thinking of you when I baked the chocolate chip cookies..."

Now here's the cool part. You will almost immediately feel a connection to them.

And why do you feel that connection? Because love never dies. They are there, around you and with you.

Many people report that they feel a strong presence, while others feel physical touches.

But it gets better!

How To Have A Conversation

"You have two ears and one mouth. Use them equally." Unknown

ASK and LISTEN:

A conversation is a two-way street. And naturally, if you have a live person in front of you, they are likely to comment and talk back to you.

So how do you hear your deceased loved one?

The answer is that you will hear them in your own mind!

No, I'm not joking. Bear with me for a minute.

When you chat, feel free to ask them how they are doing, and feel free to ask them for input into what's going on in your life.

I recommend that you keep it very light-hearted the first few times you do this. As you progress, you can certainly ask heavier questions, but for your first few times I suggest you keep it very light.

For example, I'm currently touring and I'm writing this from my hotel room. There are several great restaurants nearby. So to keep it light, I can ask my loved one where I should go for dinner.

Connect and ask. Wait for an answer or reply to pop in your head.

At first you might think that you're just imagining this or even making it up yourself. And that's fine. Proceed anyway. I will show you how the validations will come.

In the above example where I ask about the restaurants, I might get a reply like "steakhouse."

Here's what's really interesting and fun about this: the answers will often pop in quickly and decisively, even if you're indecisive at the moment.

Also, the answers you receive in this conversation may be from a different viewpoint than you currently hold.

As you practice with this, you'll start to discover the difference between your own mental voice and the voice of others.

Keep the conversation brief and upbeat. I encourage people to stick to one basic topic. This is not a time to interrogate the deceased.

Please also remember the rule that your guides guide you and your loved ones love you. This is important as many people make the mistake of seeking out their loved ones for direction in their lives when, in fact, that is not their role.

With that said, your loved ones absolutely want to communicate with you and are definitely watching over you, and they wish to continuously be a part of your life.

How do I know I am not making this up?

Truthfully, the first couple times you do this, you will not know whether you were making this up or not. And that's understandable.

There are a few clues. The first is that you will hear words and expressions that you wouldn't necessarily normally use. The expressions, in fact, will likely be expressions your loved one would've used.

The second clue is that, just like in a real conversation with a live person, your deceased loved one may have a view different than yours. If you were making it up, you'd likely agree with yourself, wouldn't you?

Concluding the session

Do you know how sometimes when you're having a conversation with somebody, the conversation lulls and you know it's time to go? Or if you're on the phone, you know it's time to hang up? In other words, the conversation is done.

It's the same here. There are no hard and fast rules for how long this conversation can go. My conversations tend to go very quickly, typically about five minutes long. For others, it may be ten to fifteen minutes.

The secret is to keep it as short and sweet as possible and to enjoy the process. Then conclude in this manner...

One - I thank the person whom I'm connecting with for spending time with me.

Two - I tell them I love them and say goodbye.

Three - I finish by doing a two-minute mindful breathing exercise, holding onto and cherishing the feeling of the messages that I have received.

When I'm done, I almost always take immediate action on any information that I've been given. If I'm supposed to call somebody, I call them. If I'm supposed to do something, I do it.

I feel this is extremely important and a great way to validate and appreciate our love ones on the other side. Think about it. They've just come through from the other side to give you information to act on! Why would you not value it?

KNOW:

Validations often come through after your session is over. They typically come quickly, though in some cases they may take a few days.

But the thing that I call "The eraser" of the doubt is the validations that you will receive.

Just like we discussed in the signs section of this book, these conversations usually bring with them signs from the other side.

Know this: your loved ones understand you will have some doubt and that you will question the validity of the conversation, so they will have absolutely no problem backing it up with other signs.

In this case, the signs will often be related to the con-versation at hand. For example, one of my clients excitedly told me that she was having a conversation with her father and that she had a leaky tap. She was unsure who to call now that he was gone. Her father was a plumber.

For some reason she felt she had to look at her fridge and, upon doing so, noticed a magnet holding a sheet of paper. The magnet was an advertisement for a local plumber!

Now as silly as that might sound, I can tell you firsthand that I have magnets on my refrigerator and I don't have a clue what they are advertisements for!

But here's the best part. She procrastinated and didn't take action on it. Later, when she had to pick up her child from school, she backed out of her garage and her toilet plunger was lying on its side in the corner of the garage!

"Blair, my toilet plunger was one of those small red ones with the short handle. They don't just accidentally fall over!"

And it's true! Those toilet plungers are darn near impossible to knock over... how weird is that?

Well, it's not weird at all. If that wasn't a validation, I don't know what is.

The validations may not come through quickly. It may take a couple of days for a validation to come through, and that's fine. Just flow with it.

The whole idea behind these connections is not to get information from spirit but to know that your loved ones are still alive in spirit. It's about them showing you they're still okay, period.

Some tips and suggestions

When you have a conversation with your loved one, by all means use your imagination at first to help you the first few times. I know of one widow who walks down to a favourite park bench of her and her husband near a canal. She brings out a photo of him and has a quiet conversation with him, something she thoroughly enjoys. She says she has a hard time doing it without the photograph, and all I can say is do what works!

The first time you do this you'll probably feel weird, awkward, and even doubt the feedback that you receive. That's perfectly okay. Your loved ones on the other side know this and they will work to help you through it.

You'll know you've had a connection because you'll feel a profound sense of peace after you have completed the session.

While it's perfectly okay to tell them you miss them and some of the challenges that you're having, it's inappropriate to spend a lot of time 'dumping' on them. They probably wouldn't have accepted that while they were living and I doubt very much they'd be happy with you doing that now that they've passed.

You will be very tempted to use this as a crutch. These connections are meant to be used sparingly. There is no time limit and no rules, per se, but I can assure you that if you do this daily, you'll be doing it too much. As a rule of thumb I recommend doing it no more than weekly, and also be prepared that they occasionally may not answer you.

This is not a rejection of you, so don't take it that way. It just might mean that they're not prepared to communicate with you on that particular day. When this happens, send your love, disconnect, and look forward to communicating on another day. Remember this works most of the time, not all of the time. They will connect with you when it's appropriate for them to do so. Trust in this. Have faith.

Conclusion

You now have three unique ways to connect with your deceased loved ones on the other side.

My best advice is to start by becoming more aware of the signs that they use to show us they are around. It's fun to get messages from our loved ones as they continue to watch us and love us.

Love never dies.

If you have a special date, such as an anniversary, I strongly suggest you try the dream connection. It's easy and works well.

Of course, having a nice TALK every now and then is awesome too.

I look forward to hearing of your successes and wish you love and light.

Blair Robertson

FREE BONUS DOWNLOAD

If you would like a FREE white light meditation downloadable audio recorded by author Blair Robertson designed to easily and effortlessly help protect you, then please visit
www.BlairRobertson.com/AfterlifeBonus

About The Author

Blair Robertson is a world-renowned psychic medium dedicated to demonstrating that love never dies, and that Spirit is all around us. Based in Phoenix, Arizona, he lives with his wife Wendy, the love of his life.

Blair has been featured on the Discovery Channel, Fox News, NBC, ABC, and hundreds of radio shows worldwide. He has produced a number of CDs, DVDs, and free online seminars on spiritual subjects.

Blair Robertson tours widely, giving demonstrations of communication with the afterlife. He was once branded a "comedium" by one of his fans for his sense of humor and compassion. Blair excels in delivering messages of love in a loving way.

He has a weekly inspirational newsletter, and we invite you to visit and subscribe at **http://www.BlairRobertson.com**

Other Books By
Blair Robertson

Blair Robertson is the best selling author of several books on a number of spiritual topics.

You can discover his books by visiting www.BlairRobertson.com/books

93637396R00052

Made in the USA
Columbia, SC
16 April 2018